STEM Jobs with
The Environment

Julie K. Lundgren

rourkeeducationalmedia.com

Scan for Related Titles
and Teacher Resources

Before Reading:

Building Academic Vocabulary and Background Knowledge

Before reading a book, it is important to tap into what your child or students already know about the topic. This will help them develop their vocabulary, increase their reading comprehension, and make connections across the curriculum.

1. Look at the cover of the book. What will this book be about?
2. What do you already know about the topic?
3. Let's study the Table of Contents. What will you learn about in the book's chapters?
4. What would you like to learn about this topic? Do you think you might learn about it from this book? Why or why not?
5. Use a reading journal to write about your knowledge of this topic. Record what you already know about the topic and what you hope to learn about the topic.
6. Read the book.
7. In your reading journal, record what you learned about the topic and your response to the book.
8. After reading the book complete the activities below.

Content Area Vocabulary
Read the list. What do these words mean?

biomass
collectively
deforestation
diversity
efficient
fossil fuels
green
old growth
ozone
precautions
sustainable
turbine

After Reading:

Comprehension and Extension Activity

After reading the book, work on the following questions with your child or students in order to check their level of reading comprehension and content mastery.

1. How do scientists study weather from the past? (Summarize)
2. What are ways that you can reduce your carbon footprint? (Text to self connection)
3. What are the positives and negatives of fossil fuels? (Summarize)
4. If waste dumping and oils spills contaminate the water, should people and companies be allowed to use the water for recreational or business purposes? Explain. (Asking questions)
5. In what ways does technology help scientists who work to protect the environment? (Asking questions)

Extension Activity

It's important to reduce your carbon footprint but many people forget how simple it can be. Think about ways your community can help the environment. Then create a poster for your school, library, or other community building that suggests ways in which they can help the environment.

Table of Contents

A Mission to Accomplish

What does it take to be a superhero? Do you need to have special powers, like the ability to fly or great strength? Today's world is in need of everyday heroes, and they have a difficult mission: to save Earth's environment.

Our world contains over 7 billion people. Many human actions cause harm to the Earth. Our appetite for **fossil fuels** and cheap food and products contributes to problems in the areas of climate change, trash, energy, water, and **deforestation**. We need problem solvers with skills and knowledge in science, technology, engineering, and math (STEM) to help keep our Earth healthy.

Deforestation as a logging practice occurs worldwide, not just in tropical rainforests.

We need people with new ideas to make our everyday actions less harmful to Earth. We also need ideas for how to fix problems we have already created. STEM is a great source for new ideas. With new solutions to old problems in place, our actions can make a difference, from a single person to whole countries.

Chemical plant operators ensure materials and reactions process smoothly.

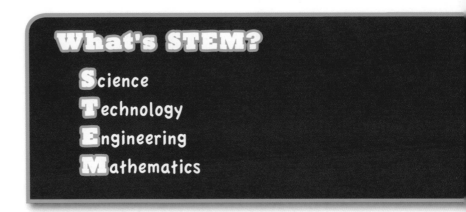

What's STEM?

Science
Technology
Engineering
Mathematics

Climate Data

People burn fossil fuels, like coal, oil, and natural gas every day. We use fossil fuels when we drive our cars, heat our homes and workplaces, and make electricity. When burned, they release carbon dioxide gas into the air. Earth's atmosphere has too much of this gas. It acts like a blanket to trap heat. The large amounts of carbon dioxide in our atmosphere cause Earth's climate to warm.

Climate change causes glaciers and polar ice caps to melt, stronger storms, and insect infestations of forests. With changing climates, habitats are lost, along with the **diversity** of plants and animals they contain.

Muir Glacier, 1892

Muir Glacier, 2005

STEM in Action!

If we add up all the ways we contribute to global climate change through the production of carbon dioxide, we come up with a measure called a carbon footprint.

Take the quiz below. Give yourself 2 points if the statement is true, 1 point if it is somewhat true, and 0 points if it is untrue.

I live in the United States.
I live in a large house.
I run electronic devices daily.
I ride in a car every day.
I rarely recycle.

What was your score? Can you think of any ways to reduce your score?

Climatologists study Earth's climate. They measure air and ocean temperatures. They compare today's data to past measurements. They find climate evidence in ice cores, tree rings, and soil deposits. Climatologists use computer models to study data and predict future climate trends. Through asking questions, conducting experiments, and collecting data, these scientists learn about climate change.

Environmental activists share information about climate change and other environmental problems. They speak and write about how to help stop climate change and repair its damage.

Climatologists and environmental activists give people the information they need to understand climate change.

A climatologist takes a soil sample.

★ Jühnde, Germany

STEM Spotlight: One Town's Solution

Jühnde, Germany is a small village that has taken its electricity and heat production into its own hands. The residents have **collectively** invested in a new community system that uses **biomass** instead of fossil fuels. Engineers designed a system that uses manure and grains for fuel. The small power plant produces enough energy for about 140 households. It then sells any extra power it has produced to traditional electric companies.

Cow manure and waste wood are common sources of biomass.

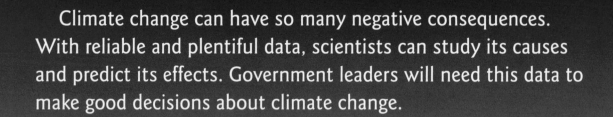

Climate change can have so many negative consequences. With reliable and plentiful data, scientists can study its causes and predict its effects. Government leaders will need this data to make good decisions about climate change.

Glaciers in the Mt. Everest region have shrunk by 13 percent in the last 50 years due to climate change.

Real STEM Job: *Sustainability Director*

Many corporations have made it their mission to reduce their carbon footprint and become more **sustainable**. A sustainability director leads the way toward this goal. Sustainability directors look at waste management, energy use, and production. They use math to analyze the inefficiencies and research new technology or new practices that are better for the environment.

STEM Fast Fact: McDonald's and L'Oreal are two American companies with sustainability directors.

Planners and supervisors at sewage treatment plants are responsible for running efficient and clean operations.

Trash Problems

People create a lot of trash. Scientists estimate that each person in the U.S. creates 102 tons (93 metric tons) of trash in his or her lifetime. This weight is equal to seven or eight school buses fully loaded with passengers and fuel.

To get rid of our trash, we may truck it to an incinerator or a landfill. Incinerators burn trash, but produce gases that contribute to climate change and air pollution. Landfills cause problems, too.

Waste incineration plants produce toxic ash that contains heavy metals, an environmental concern.

In a landfill, trash is buried. Landfills are designed to keep the trash in place. Landfill engineers tell workers that the trash must be buried in giant, plastic-lined holes. When full, the holes are covered with soil, clay, plastic, more soil, and living plants. These layers help stop trash from seeping into the ground.

But trash doesn't always stay where it is supposed to be. Despite these **precautions**, many landfills still pollute ground water with toxic chemicals and heavy metals and give off bad odors. Landfills also occupy valuable land that could have been used for buildings, farms, or parks.

Modern landfills typically begin with a lining of high density polyethylene (HDPE) plastic to protect the surrounding environment.

STEM in Action!

You can estimate the amount of trash your town produces.

First, find out the population of the town or city in which you live. Now multiply that number by 102 tons of garbage.

New York City has 8.3 million people.

$8.3 \times 102 = 846.6$ million tons of garbage.

Where will all this garbage go? We need new ideas for ways to get rid of our trash.

Reducing waste is key to solving the world's trash problem. Not creating waste in the first place is much better than figuring out what to do with the waste once it is created. Coming up with new ways to reuse and recycle materials keeps them out of landfills, too.

Recycled materials may be used to manufacture new products.

STEM Fast Fact:

Aluminum cans may be recycled easily with less cost and energy than mining new aluminum. The soda cans you recycle can be turned into new soda cans in about 60 days.

Real STEM Job: *Metallurgist*

Some items are relatively easy to recycle. Stainless-steel cans, for example, can be sent right back to the steel mill to be used in other steel products. But some materials require more work. Figuring out how to turn an aluminum can into something new is not so simple.

Chemical engineers and metallurgists work together to perfect recycling methods for aluminum cans and other metals. They come up with methods to remove paint and labels, remove impurities from the metal, and reform the metal. Similar research and planning is necessary for recycling any material, whether paper, plastic, or something else.

Metallurgists use heat to purify recycled metals.

Chemical engineers design, construct, and operate chemical plants.

Green Energy Solutions

The world relies on fossil fuels to provide energy for transportation, electricity, manufacturing, and heating and cooling buildings. But fossil fuels pollute the Earth and cause climate change. And their supply is limited. Our energy appetite demands more fuel each year. We need engineers, scientists, and technology workers to build systems that use renewable sources of energy.

Engineers design and build clean energy production solutions, such as panel systems.

Solar power uses the Sun's heat to create electricity. Engineers have designed various ways to capture solar power. Sometimes they use sunlight and a system of mirrors to heat liquids that power electric generators. Other methods use solar panels to directly convert sunlight into electricity.

However, with current technology, not every city gets enough sunlight for it to be a good place to capture solar energy. Engineers are always working to build better, more **efficient**, and less expensive methods to collect solar energy.

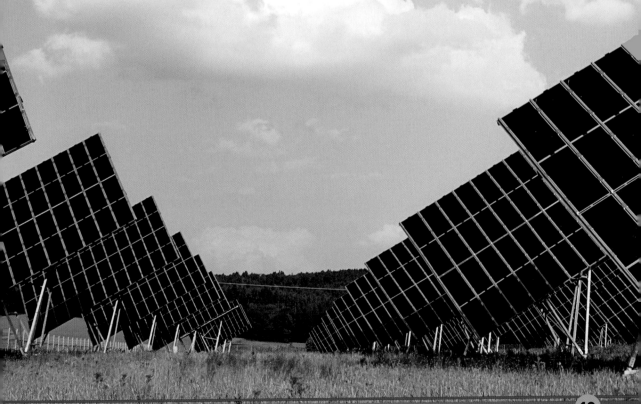

Engineers have also designed towering modern windmills that use rotating blades shaped like airplane wings. As the blades spin, they turn a shaft and feed the energy into an electric generator inside the **turbine**. A generator converts the mechanical energy into electric energy. Every piece works together to get the most power from the wind.

A lot of planning goes into the placement of wind farms as well. Someone has to scout out the areas that get a good amount of wind. They must measure the wind on ridges, fields, and seas and compare the locations. Then they choose a spot that will also not disturb people living nearby. Many people dislike wind farms for their looks and noise.

Wind turbine blades can be up to 150 feet (46 meters) long, about as long as nine medium cars parked bumper to bumper.

STEM in Action!

Evaluate your home for **green** energy alternatives.

Would your home be a good candidate for solar panels? Monitor the amount of sunlight your home gets. Do trees block sunlight from falling on your roof? Is there another location for solar panels?

How about wind? Research how to go about evaluating your home's potential for wind power. What kind of space and equipment do you need? Are windmills permitted in your area?

The expense of developing and building renewable energy systems will cost hundreds of millions of dollars. But the cost of continuing to use fossil fuels must include the cost of fixing the environmental damage to our planet. The rich variety of STEM jobs created by the development and use of renewable energy has the potential to help the Earth and support workers and their families.

Geothermal power plants take advantage of the fact that Earth's internal heat is always available, unlike solar energy that relies on sunlight.

Real STEM Job: *Geothermal Power Generation Engineer*

Geothermal power taps naturally occurring heat energy by drilling deep into the Earth's crust in places where heat sources are closer to the surface.

Accessing these areas requires a skilled geothermal power generation engineer. These engineers are responsible for designing the machines that will access and tap into the heat source. They must take a great number of variables into consideration for their designs. Because geothermal heat is deep below Earth's surface, they must design tools that can withstand the intense heat and pressure. The tools also need to be operated from the surface.

Geothermal power requires many other important STEM skills as well. People with special knowledge about geology, computer modeling, drilling and mining engineering, and manufacturing will help lead the way to geothermal power.

Iceland and more than 20 other countries use geothermal power.

Cleaner Waters

A heavily oiled Kemp's Ridley turtle was found at the Deepwater Horizon accident site in 2010.

In the Pacific Ocean, discarded and lost items float on an area three times the size of Texas.

We need clean water for drinking and growing food crops. We also need our oceans and shorelines clean for fish and other sea life. Much of our water contains fertilizer, metals, toxic chemicals, and traces of medications. Oil spills and waste dumping contaminate the fish and other animals that live in the water. Water shortages affect many areas as well, including over 30 U.S. states.

STEM jobs related to water conservation and water quality provide excellent career opportunities. Workers skilled in computer programming can engineer and manage water control systems.

Environmental analysts can monitor water quality in various habitats, collect and report data, and help develop rules that support good water management.

Hydrologists study the science of Earth's water. They use science and math to help solve our planet's water problems. Whether you like to work inside or outside, a job waits for you.

Workers sampling potentially hazardous waters often wear personal protective equipment (PPE) such as waterproof suits, masks, gloves, and hardhats.

STEM in Action!

Oceanographer Dr. Curt Ebbesmeyer became interested in studying ocean currents through the use of floating cargo lost at sea. He called his study of the motion of this ocean **flotsam,** "flotsametrics." By tracking lost cargo like shoes and tub toys, he has learned how the ocean moves our trash and how long it takes to disintegrate.

Conduct your own flotsam study.

First, partly fill a tub or kid's plastic pool with water.

To generate a current, stir the pool or submerge a running garden hose in the water.

Now, drop old sneakers, tub toys, plastic balls, plastic bags, or other floaters into the water.

Observe what happens to each object. How does it move? Is it on top of the water or partly under water? What happens when the current stops?

Earth's oceans contain about eight significant patches of flotsam, much of it plastic. What's floating on the oceans is largely unexplored. How do we clean it up? What problems does it create for sea life?

World Wind Patterns

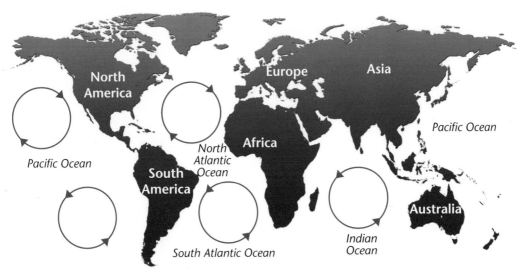

Five major areas of circular wind patterns act like a sweeping broom to swirl floating objects into concentrated areas.

An international organization of beachcombers helps Dr. Ebbesmeyer find lost cargo, like the bath toys and Nike shoes he first tracked. This data helps him create computer models of the ocean's currents.

Real STEM Job: *Hydrologist*

Hydrologists play many different roles in water management. By studying rainfall records, snow amounts, and river flows, they help cities know if their water supply is enough to meet their needs. They manage reservoirs and dams and decide how much water to store or release from the reservoir.

Some hydrologists monitor water quality in area lakes and rivers. When water is not safe for swimming or fishing, they alert people to the danger. Many times, when water is unsafe, the contaminant will disperse and water levels will be within a safe range. But when assistance is needed to clean the water, hydrologists may lead clean-up projects or pollution prevention programs.

Hydrologist Martha Nielsen, of the United States Geological Survey (USGS), examines samples as a crew works to drill a new monitoring well at a USGS station near Middle Dam on Lower Richardson Lake in Maine.

Managing Forests

In countries with high population growth and high resource needs, people threaten whole ecosystems. The demand for lumber, charcoal, and farmland endangers rainforests and other **old growth** forests. Tropical rainforests hold a natural treasure of plants and animals. Once destroyed, we cannot create these forests again.

Plants and trees in rainforests and other forest ecosystems help stabilize Earth's climate by taking up carbon dioxide and producing oxygen.

Scientists use satellite photos taken over time to estimate the rate and amount of rainforest lost each year. They estimate that 38,600 square miles (100,000 square kilometers) disappear annually.

Forest conservation workers help protect and manage forests. They may study the impact, prevention, and spread of tree diseases and insect problems. They may direct tree harvests to minimize habitat damage and plant new trees. They study the role that fire plays in forest management. They try to understand the relationship between forest size and habitat quality.

Fire can renew forests by opening up areas to sunlight and burning dead materials. However, when fires are also used to clear land for other uses, such as building or agriculture, the benefits are lost.

STEM in Action!

Google Earth is an online database of satellite photographs of Earth put together to form a continuous map. Google Earth allows you to zoom in quite close and see detail.

If you have access to the Internet and a computer, search Google Earth for an area of tropical rainforest in South America near the equator. You should be able to pinpoint areas of current logging.

Save screenshots of the areas. A month later return to the site and see if satellite photos have been updated.

Using the map's scale, can you estimate how large of an area has been logged?

Satellite photos make excellent tools for monitoring deforestation in places like the Amazon rainforest in Brazil.

Real STEM Job: *Forest Restoration Project Manager*

When forests have been eliminated or damaged by overharvesting, a Forest Restoration Project Manager steps in to recreate and renew the forest. The duties range from project planning and choosing trees to plant, to working with local, state, and federal governments to get necessary permits and approvals.

The project manager must know about the environment he or she is trying to recreate. They must also have a great understanding of the roles different plants and animals have in the ecosystem. To create a thriving forest, all the plants and animals that live there must have what they need to thrive. The process takes a long time. A project manager will work with a team over many years to carry out the plan so that a healthy forest will grow.

Pollution Response

Pollution is a common occurrence in our natural environments. Many beautiful nature areas are destroyed by pollution every year. Industries may dump waste where they are not supposed to. Rainwater will sometimes carry unwanted chemicals to previously uncontaminated areas.

Environmental scientists help identify polluted areas. They visit sites that people have identified as possibly polluted. The scientists test the soil and the water. They take samples from plant and animal life. Seeing how pollution has affected animals can tell the scientists how big of a problem pollution is in the area.

Pollution from traffic and factories regularly reduces Hong Kong's air quality to a point where it increases health risks.

Once a problem is identified, environmental specialists come up with solutions. They identify the source of the pollution and figure out how to put a stop to it. They clean the water and the soil. They may even treat sick animals.

Environmental specialists sample sources to find pollution and monitor its cleanup.

STEM in Action!

With the right tools, it is easy to test your water's pH level. The water's pH level tells how acidic or basic the water is. Mining, burning fossil fuels, and industrial waste can lower water's pH to a point where it is unsafe for fish and other animals.

To test water's pH level, you need pH strips, which are available at drug stores.

First, get a clean glass for your sample. Fill the glass and allow the water to settle.

Then, dip the paper into the water. The paper will turn color. Compare the paper to the chart on the container. It will tell you the pH of the water.

If you suspect your water is contaminated with something dangerous, find a professional. Different tests are necessary to identify the different possible contaminants.

Dip the tip of the pH paper into your sample for a few seconds.

Compare the paper to the color chart. It will tell you the pH reading.

Prevention is also an important part of the pollution response. By educating people about the negative effects of pollution, it is possible to reverse damage. In the 1990s, scientists linked aerosol spray cans to the depleting **ozone** layer. People responded by not using aerosols. Manufacturers soon removed ozone depleting chemicals from aerosols in the U.S. This pollution response helped stop the destruction of the ozone layer.

Today's aerosols no longer contain CFCs, the chemicals that contribute to ozone depletion.

Real STEM Job: *Environmental Chemist*

In addition to working in the field, many environmental chemists work for chemical companies. They make sure that the chemicals the company uses are safe for people and the environment. Environmental chemists pay particular attention to how a company gets rid of its waste. They make sure the chemicals are disposed of correctly and according to government rules.

Many times, a company will hire an environmental chemist after it has done something to pollute the environment. The company will hire a chemist to figure out how to clean up and restore the environment.

Environmental chemists carry out work with chemicals, manufacturing processes, and proper and safe waste disposal.

STEM for the Future

With so many worldwide environmental problems, we need the talents, knowledge, and experience of STEM workers to help find smart solutions. Our future depends on solving these big problems quickly, and not just one person or home at a time. By working together on a large scale and using all our STEM knowledge, we can meet today's environmental challenges and opportunities.

Solar energy engineers and installation specialists supervise and study solar panel projects, collecting data to improve technologies.

STEM Job Fact Sheets

Sustainability Director

Important Skills: Complex Problem-Solving, Judgment and Decision Making, Critical Thinking, Environmental Science, Communications

Important Knowledge: Administration and Management, Economics, Law and Government, Environmental Science

College Major: Business Administration and Management, Public Administration, Finance

Median Salary: $165,000

Metallurgist

Important Skills: Active Listening, Critical Thinking, Reading Comprehension, Speaking, Complex Problem-Solving

Important Knowledge: Engineering and Technology, Chemistry, Mathematics, Physics

College Major: Materials Engineering, Metallurgical Engineering, Polymer/Plastics Engineering

Median Salary: $85,860

Geothermal Power Generation Engineer

Important Skills: Attention to Detail, Analytical Thinking, Dependability, Initiative, Persistence

Important Knowledge: Complex Problem-Solving, Critical Thinking, Mathematics, Reading Comprehension, Active Listening

College Major: Electromechanical Engineering, Mechanical Engineering

Median Salary: $82,480

Hydrologist

Important Skills: Critical Thinking, Reading Comprehension, Science, Mathematics, Communication

Important Knowledge: Mapping, Mathematics, Engineering and Technology, Physics, Chemistry, Geography

College Major: Hydrology, Chemistry, Oceanography

Median Salary: $75,500

Forest Restoration Project Manager

Important Skills: Critical Thinking, Teamwork, Judgment and Decision Making, Monitoring, Listening

Important Knowledge: Administration and Management, Biology, Geography, Mathematics, Economics

College Major: Ecology, Biology, Environmental Studies

Median Salary: $59,310

Environmental Chemist

Important Skills: Science, Analytical Skills, Critical Thinking, Problem-Solving, Speaking

Important Knowledge: Chemistry, Mathematics, Computers and Electronics, Production and Processing

College Major: Environmental Science, Chemistry

Median Salary: $73,240

Glossary

biomass (BYE-oh-mass): plant or animal material used as fuel

collectively (kuh-LEK-tiv-lee): as a group

deforestation (dee-for-iss-TAY-shun): removal of trees from an area

diversity (di-VUR-si-tee): being different or having differences

efficient (i-FISH-uhnt): able to work with minimum use of energy, time, money, or materials

flotsam (FLAHT-sum): floating debris including lost items, trash, and natural materials like tree branches and leaves

fossil fuels (FAH-suhl FYU-uhls): stored energy formed millions of years ago from the remains of plants and animals

green (GREEN): helpful, healthy and safe for the environment and the Earth

old growth (OHLD GROHTH): original, never before disturbed by humans

ozone (OH-zone): a colorless atmospheric gas that forms a protective layer around Earth, screening harmful solar radiation

precautions (prah-KAW-shuhns): measures taken beforehand to ensure success

sustainable (suh-STAYN-uh-buhl): able to maintain itself

turbine (TER-bine): a machine with a spinning blade that turns a rotor to produce energy

Index

Show What You Know

1. How do fossil fuels contribute to climate change?
2. What STEM fields does a sustainability director need to understand?
3. How can STEM knowledge help clean and protect our water?
4. Why does the author include an activity using Google Earth to monitor forests?
5. Why is solar energy not always the best green energy source?

Websites to Visit

dnr.wi.gov/eek/

www.ecokids.ca/pub/homework_help/index.cfm

epa.gov/climatechange/kids/index.html

About the Author

Julie K. Lundgren carries a deep fascination for plants, animals, and science about the natural environment. She always has great ideas for Nature Adventure Days, in which her family reluctantly participates, but afterward they are always glad they did. Ms. Lundgren gets inspiration from her beloved Minnesota, home of many large mosquitoes, muskies, and potholes.

Meet The Author!
www.meetREMauthors.com

www.rourkeeducationalmedia.com

PHOTO CREDITS: Title Page © StockRocket; page 4 © emicristea; page 5 © Kali Nice LLC; page 6 © Nikita Sobolkov, Harry Fileding and Bruce F. Molnia: National Snow and Ice Data Center/The Glacier Photograph Collection; page 7 © Elena Elisseeva; page 8 © BartCo; page 9 © Jason Register, Sara Winter; page 10 © bbuong; page 11 © antikainen; page 12 ©Anagramm; page 13 © Joruba; page 14 © Inga Nielson; page 15 © Steve Debenport, Fotofermer; page 16 © Max Maro; page 17 © 06photo; page 18 © goodluz; page 19 © manfredxy; page 20 © Redro Antonio Salaverría Calahorra; page 21 © brainmaster (inset), © acilo; page 22 © LS KAHLE 4FR PHOTOGRAPHY; page 23 © Johann Ragnarsson; page 24 © Carolyn Cole/LA Times, Vasiliki Varvaki; page 25 © microgen; page 27 © Thumb, Dr. Curt Ebbesmeyer; page 29 © Scott Bendtson; page 30 © Fred Froese; page 31 © Samir Arora; page 33 © Marie Liss, Google Earth; page 35 © George Clerk; page 36 © Nicontiger; page 37 © Bart Co; page 38 © Deyan Georgiev, Sudo2; page 39 © nicola margaret; page 40 © Miodrage Gajic; page 41 © Jim Jurca; page 42 © jianghaistudio; page 43 © LL28

Edited by: Jill Sherman

Cover design by: Tara Raymo
Interior design by: Renee Brady

Library of Congress PCN Data

STEM Jobs with the Environment / Julie K. Lundgren
(STEM Jobs You'll Love)
ISBN 978-1-62717-697-2 (hard cover)
ISBN 978-1-62717-819-8 (soft cover)
ISBN 978-1-62717-933-1 (e-Book)
Library of Congress Control Number: 2014935489

Printed in the United States of America, North Mankato, Minnesota

Also Available as:

ROURKE'S
e-Books